C000182451

Published in 2010 by
The Original Double Red Ltd
4 Gateway Court
Dankerwood Road
South Hykeham
Lincoln LN6 9UL

Tel: +44 (0)1522 693 278
www.doublered.co.uk

ISBN 978-0-9534420-7-2

Photography and Copyright of all images
Double Red

Photographers
James Wright
Keith Lock
Sue Ward
Dave Yeomans
Chippy Wood
Rob Hodgson
David Reygondeau
Graham Holt

Project Manager
Sue Ward

Picture Editors
James Wright
Sue Ward
Katie Ward

Contributors
Dave Fern
Sue Jobling
Phil Wain

Contributing Editor
Larry Carter

Design and Layout
Katie Ward

Results and Statistics
Timing Solutions Ltd. www.tsl-timing.com

Special Thanks to:
The organisers and sponsors involved in the MCE Insurance British Superbike Series,
especially the team at MSVR, whose dedication and commitment makes the MCE British
Insurance Superbike Championship the strongest domestic championship in the world.
Every single person involved in the organisation and running of the championship whose
often difficult jobs go unnoticed and unrewarded - they know who they are - the medics,
physios, marshals, press officers, scrutineers, journalists, television crews, truck drivers,
mechanics, chefs, cleaners, hospitality crews, commentators etc and last but not least the
riders and teams, who seldom complain at 'just one more shot' and make the MCE
Insurance British Superbike Championship the amazing spectacle it is.

All Rights Reserved:
No part of this publication may be reproduced in a retrieval system, or transmitted in any
form or by any means, electronic, mechanical, photocopying, recording, or otherwise,
without the prior written permission of The Original Double Red Ltd. While every effort has
been made to ensure the accuracy of the facts and data contained in this publication, no
responsibility can be accepted by The Original Double Red Ltd or any of the contributors
for errors or omissions, or their consequences.

All the images in this book are available as custom prints. For enquiries please contact
Double Red at the above address.

© 2010 The Original Double Red Ltd

Contents

"I think 90$^{\%}$ of motorcycle racing is between the ears"

- Kevin Schwantz

Foreword
Seeing Red 2010

The 2010 MCE Insurance British Superbike Championship will surely be considered a vintage season in years to come. Of course as well as the jaw dropping racing much attention focused on the raft of rule changes brought in pre-season, the most talked about being the new points system, which ultimately did what it was designed to do, throwing up multiple scenarios and taking the championship down to the final race of the final event.

With less attention but of more overall importance the BSB-Evolution class was born. Six manufacturers were represented in a class which will surely define the future path of Superbike racing.

At the end of twenty six enthralling races the mercurial talent that is Japan's Ryuichi Kiyonari dealt the killer blow with three masterly controlled race wins, capitalising on his nearest rivals' misfortunes. He now takes his place in BSB history equalling Niall Mackenzie and John Reynolds' triple crowns.

As the long winter draws in it's good to be able to sit back and review the season through the lens of Double Red and also comparing to previous years editions it's great to see that BSB Champions and race winners are now populating World Championship paddocks with some success.

With careful navigation the series goes from strength to strength supported by a hugely committed community of riders, teams, sponsors, the media and my organising colleagues. My thanks to them and of course the BSB fans who watch their heroes in their droves week in and week out trackside and on television.

Roll on April 2011 and we start all over again.

Stuart Higgs
Series Director

Ryuichi Kiyonari

HM Plant Honda

After two years away on World Superbike duty, it was back to domestic action for the former British Champion who had previously lifted the crown for HM Plant Honda in 2006 and 2007. However, it wasn't all plain sailing for the 28-year-old Japanese ace and, apart from a first race podium at Brands Hatch over Easter, following a combination of mechanical problems and lack of form, it looked as though his bid for a third crown would be flawed early on. But Kiyo stuck at it and soon he was racking up the wins and podiums and looking good as he went into the Showdown stage of the season. Despite a hiccup at Croft, and not being overly inspiring at Silverstone, three impressive victories at the final round at Oulton netted him his hat trick of British Superbike Championships to match Niall Mackenzie's record set way back in the 1990s.

Results	
Position:	1
Points:	649
Swan Combi Poles:	2
Fastest Lap Poles:	4
Front Rows:	12
Best Grid:	Pole
Races:	26
Wins:	7
Podiums:	9
Best Result:	1st
Fastest Laps:	6

R1	Brands Hatch Indy:	2nd + R	
R2	Thruxton:	9th + 4th	
R3	Oulton Park:	R + 4th	
R4	Cadwell:	1st + R	
R5	Mallory Park:	1st + 1st	
R6	Knockhill:	2nd	
R7	Snetterton:	2nd + R + 1st	
R8	Brands Hatch GP:	3rd + 2nd + 2nd	
R9	**Cadwell:**	**3rd + 3rd**	
R10	Croft:	11th + 4th	
R11	Silverstone:	5th + 2nd	
R12	Oulton:	1st + 1st + 1st	

Josh Brookes
HM Plant Honda

Following his somewhat eventful debut season in BSB in 2009, the 27-year-old Aussie dubbed 'Bad Boy' by certain elements had much to prove and was many people's tip for top honours especially by staying with the HM Plant Honda team. Apart from blotting his copybook with a crash in the season opener, Brookesy proved to be the model of relative inconsistency in the opening salvos as he combined brilliance with frustration. However, from mid season onwards he started looking like a proper title contender, and briefly held the series lead. Qualifying easily as a Title Fighter, the Showdown proved his nemesis as he failed to muster a win and only stepped onto the podium in 50% of those races and as a result had to settle for runner-up spot behind his team mate.

Results	
Position:	2
Points:	625
Swan Combi Poles:	3
Fastest Lap Poles:	3
Front Rows:	9
Best Grid:	Pole
Races:	26
Wins:	5
Podiums:	9
Best Result:	1st
Fastest Laps:	6

R1	Brands Hatch Indy:	5th + C
R2	Thruxton:	2nd + 1st
R3	Oulton Park:	6th + 8th
R4	Cadwell:	5th + 1st
R5	Mallory Park:	2nd + 2nd
R6	Knockhill:	3rd
R7	Snetterton:	1st + 1st + R
R8	Brands Hatch GP:	4th + C + 6th
R9	Cadwell:	2nd + 1st
R10	Croft:	6th + 8th
R11	Silverstone:	2nd + 3rd
R12	Oulton:	5th + 3rd + 2nd

Tommy Hill
Worx Crescent Suzuki

A season which promised so much ended in a tearful finale as England's big hope for BSB honours literally crashed and burned at the final hurdle. The 25-year-old Londoner was in command of the championship for much of the year and even when the Worx Suzuki had problems, he somehow ground out a result to lead the series going into the Showdown. He got off to a great start at Croft and although he failed to deliver at Silverstone 'Rock On Tommy' was red-hot favourite arriving at Oulton. After a podium in race one, the drama unfolded in the meanest of fashions as he crashed out spectacularly in race two, the machine catching fire in the process, effectively ending his title aspirations. It was very hard luck on the home crowd's favourite but it just wasn't destined to be his season. Expect him to be back - stronger than ever.

Results	
Position:	3
Points:	620
Swan Combi Poles:	6
Fastest Lap Poles:	2
Front Rows:	8
Best Grid:	Pole
Races:	26
Wins:	4
Podiums:	11
Best Result:	1st
Fastest Laps:	4

R1	Brands Hatch Indy:	1st + 2nd
R2	Thruxton:	1st + 2nd
R3	Oulton Park:	2nd + 3rd
R4	Cadwell:	C + 2nd
R5	Mallory Park:	R + 8th
R6	Knockhill:	8th
R7	Snetterton:	3rd + 2nd + 2nd
R8	Brands Hatch GP:	15th + 6th + 4th
R9	Cadwell:	1st + 2nd
R10	Croft:	1st + 2nd
R11	Silverstone:	8th + 5th
R12	Oulton:	2nd + C + 5th

Michael Laverty
Relentless Suzuki by TAS

Not many people would have had the elder of the Laverty brothers down as a major title contender this term, especially after a few seasons away from BSB and having spent last year in relative obscurity on the AMA and world stage. But they don't come much more focused than the 29-year-old Ulsterman and people started to take notice after a win in the wet at Oulton was followed up by four successive dry podiums. There or thereabouts when he needed to be, he qualified for the Showdown despite a crash at Brands and after a great win at Croft, his hopes went west with his sliding Suzuki at Silverstone in the wet. Still, a top four placing in the series is a brilliant achievement for both Michael and the Relentless TAS team of which they should be proud.

Results	
Position:	4
Points:	604
Swan Combi Poles:	0
Fastest Lap Poles:	1
Front Rows:	12
Best Grid:	Pole
Races:	26
Wins:	2
Podiums:	7
Best Result:	1st
Fastest Laps:	2

R1	Brands Hatch Indy:	R + 4th
R2	Thruxton:	10th + 6th
R3	Oulton Park:	5th + 1st
R4	Cadwell:	2nd + 3rd
R5	Mallory Park:	3rd + 3rd
R6	Knockhill:	4th
R7	Snetterton:	6th + 5th + 3rd
R8	Brands Hatch GP:	6th + 4th + C
R9	Cadwell:	4th + 4th
R10	Croft:	2nd + 1st
R11	Silverstone:	3rd + C
R12	Oulton:	4th + 8th + 4th

Key:						
1	Finishing Position	R	Retired	Inj.	Injured
C	Crashed	NS	Non Starter		

Michael Rutter
RidersMotorcycles.com Ducati

So many people wanted the fairytale ending to what would have been the most gripping of stories, but it wasn't to be for the veteran Brummie. Aboard the Ducati he last raced properly in 2008, Rutter was at best an outside chance to claim an odd podium this season but as the season progressed, he started to become a regular thorn in the sides of the favourites and when he won at Knockhill, in his favoured conditions it must be said, it was game on! Alas, the Showdown didn't reap the rewards and two crashes, one in the dry at Croft and the other in the damp at Silverstone ended The Blade's bid to land that elusive first ever road racing crown, for this year at least.

Results				
Position:				5
Points:				559
Swan Combi Poles:				1
Fastest Lap Poles:				2
Front Rows:				12
Best Grid:				Pole
Races:				26
Wins:				2
Podiums:				5
Best Result:				1st
Fastest Laps:				3
R1	Brands Hatch Indy:	7th + 6th		
R2	Thruxton:	5th + 7th		
R3	Oulton Park:	R + 2nd		
R4	Cadwell:	3rd + 4th		
R5	Mallory Park:	4th + 4th		
R6	Knockhill:	1st		
R7	Snetterton:	4th + R + 4th		
R8	Brands Hatch GP:	2nd + 3rd + 3rd		
R9	Cadwell:	5th + 5th		
R10	Croft:	C + 5th		
R11	Silverstone:	1st + C		
R12	Oulton:	R + 4th + R		

Alastair Seeley
Relentless Suzuki by TAS

Results		
Position:		6
Points:		550
Swan Combi Poles:		0
Fastest Lap Poles:		1
Front Rows:		3
Best Grid:		Pole
Races:		26
Wins:		1
Podiums:		2
Best Result:		1st
Fastest Laps:		2
R1	Brands Hatch Indy:	4th + 3rd
R2	Thruxton:	12th + 9th
R3	Oulton Park:	4th + 6th
R4	Cadwell:	9th + 7th
R5	Mallory Park:	10th + 11th
R6	Knockhill:	5th
R7	Snetterton:	5th + 3rd + C
R8	Brands Hatch GP:	1st + C + C
R9	Cadwell:	8th + 9th
R10	Croft:	C + 15th
R11	Silverstone:	6th + 4th
R12	Oulton:	15th + 5th + 7th

Simply sensational for the BSB rookie who was so new to it all. He'd never even raced around Mallory Park before! Twelve months after cocking his leg over an EVO bike for the Relentless team, last year's Superstock 1000 Champion was soon in the mix and scored a fantastic podium at the opening round. The Wee Wizard from Carrickfergus then went about learning his trade and continued to score well, taking an amazing victory in the wet at Brands en route to the Showdown. Lady luck then deserted the 31-year-old as he blew any hopes of the title with a disaster at Croft. As well as his prowess at the North West 200 where he took the main Superbike race, Seeley has shown enough promise to be a major BSB contender next season.

James Ellison
Swan Honda

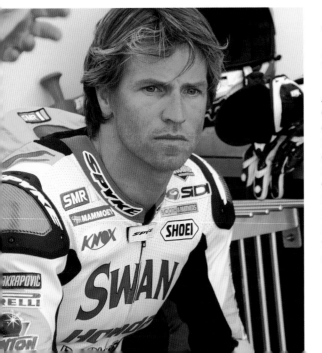

A season of what might have been for the 30-year-old Cumbrian who finished runner-up last year to his all-conquering team mate Leon Camier. Back with Shaun Muir's team under the guise of Swan Honda, the season got off to a great start with a victory and podium at Brands over Easter but then, during free practice for the very next round at Thruxton, Ellison crashed heavily and broke his leg. Although he was back just three rounds later, in truth he wasn't fit and it took until the last three rounds for the former MotoGP rider to get back to the form he is capable of and what, save for the injury, would surely have been a tilt at the title.

Results				
Position:				7
Points:				210
Swan Combi Poles:				0
Fastest Lap Poles:				0
Front Rows:				7
Best Grid:				2nd
Races:				20
Wins:				2
Podiums:				3
Best Result:				1st
Fastest Laps:				2
R1	Brands Hatch Indy:	3rd + 1st		
R2	Thruxton:	NS + NS		
R3	Oulton Park:	Inj. + Inj.		
R4	Cadwell:	Inj. + Inj.		
R5	Mallory Park:	13th + 12th		
R6	Knockhill:	R		
R7	Snetterton:	7th + 4th + C		
R8	Brands Hatch GP:	7th + 5th + 5th		
R9	Cadwell:	6th + 6th		
R10	Croft:	R + 6th		
R11	Silverstone:	4th + 1st		
R12	Oulton:	3rd + 7th + 3rd		

John Laverty
Buildbase Kawasaki

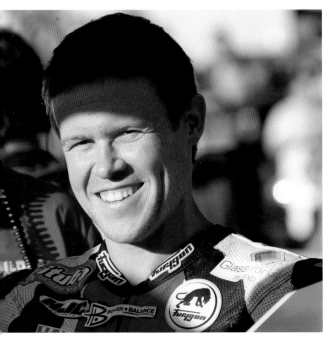

Proving points really do make prizes, Laverty very nearly made the Showdown with his remarkable consistency by finishing the first 15 races of the series in the points, only to miss out on a distant chance of qualifying for the Title Fight when he clashed with Tommy Bridewell at Cadwell. With a brilliant podium at Oulton early in the season, the 28-year-old from Toomebridge was always in the mix and it's credit to his talent and those of the Buildbase Kawasaki team that they were in with a shout right up until the end. They can be justifiably proud of a top eight placing, when you look at the calibre of riders and teams behind them.

Results	
Position:	8
Points:	190
Swan Combi Poles:	0
Fastest Lap Poles:	0
Front Rows:	0
Best Grid:	5th
Races:	26
Wins:	0
Podiums:	1
Best Result:	3rd
Fastest Laps:	0

R1	Brands Hatch Indy:	10th + 7th
R2	Thruxton:	7th + 8th
R3	Oulton Park:	3rd + 5th
R4	Cadwell:	6th + 5th
R5	Mallory Park:	8th + 6th
R6	Knockhill:	6th
R7	Snetterton:	12th + 10th + 5th
R8	Brands Hatch GP:	9th + C + 9th
R9	Cadwell:	C + 12th
R10	Croft:	8th + 13th
R11	Silverstone:	C + 9th
R12	Oulton:	9th + 6th + 8th

Stuart Easton
Swan Honda

Results	
Position:	9
Points:	189
Swan Combi Poles:	0
Fastest Lap Poles:	0
Front Rows:	5
Best Grid:	2nd
Races:	26
Wins:	1
Podiums:	4
Best Result:	1st
Fastest Laps:	0

R1	Brands Hatch Indy:	6th + 5th
R2	Thruxton:	4th + 3rd
R3	Oulton Park:	1st + R
R4	Cadwell:	C + 10th
R5	Mallory Park:	5th + R
R6	Knockhill:	R
R7	Snetterton:	R + 8th + R
R8	Brands Hatch GP:	C + 7th + 8th
R9	Cadwell:	10th + 11th
R10	Croft:	3rd + 3rd
R11	Silverstone:	R + R
R12	Oulton:	7th + 2nd + R

The season started badly for the quietly spoken Scotsman with an injury sustained during pre-season testing and after being buoyed by a win at Oulton, it got progressively worse for the 27-year-old from Hawick. A combination of machine problems and set-up issues then plagued the former Supersport Champion and by mid season, it was plain to see he was struggling with confidence. Despite his problems, Easton bounced back well with a double podium at Croft and backed that up with a fine second place in the season finale but it was all too little too late and he's moved on from the Swan Honda team to race for MSS Kawasaki next season.

Chris Walker
Sorrymate.com SMT Honda/ CW Racing/ MSS Colchester Kawasaki

You just can't keep an old dog down and once again, The Stalker confounded many of his critics by not only racing on, but proving that he was still damned competitive. Forming his own team at the start of the year as no offers were forthcoming, the 38-year-old Midlander went on to ride the MSS Kawasaki and latterly Robin Croft's SMT Honda, and what's more, he was capable of giving the leading riders a run for their money, most famously at Mallory where he was threatening a podium. Whether he's back next year remains to be seen but if not, top ten in the world's toughest domestic race series is no mean achievement!

Results	
Position:	10
Points:	130
Swan Combi Poles:	0
Fastest Lap Poles:	0
Front Rows:	0
Best Grid:	6th
Races:	26
Wins:	0
Podiums:	0
Best Result:	5th
Fastest Laps:	0

R1	Brands Hatch Indy:	9th + C
R2	Thruxton:	R + 15th
R3	Oulton Park:	8th + 11th
R4	Cadwell:	7th + 8th
R5	Mallory Park:	6th + 5th
R6	Knockhill:	10th
R7	Snetterton:	11th + 7th + 7th
R8	Brands Hatch GP:	R + R + 13th
R9	Cadwell:	11th + 15th
R10	Croft:	9th + 12th
R11	Silverstone:	9th + 8th
R12	Oulton:	R + R + 9th

HM Plant Honda

HM Plant Honda

Machinery: Honda CBR1000RR Fireblade
Manager: Havier Beltran
Located: Louth, Lincolnshire
Pedigree: British Superbike Champions 2006, 2007 & 2010

On paper, the former official Honda World Superbike Championship team looked to be the strongest in the series with both Josh Brookes and Ryuichi Kiyonari having world championship credentials.

They didn't have the best of starts to the season but eventually came good and dominated throughout the middle part of the year allowing both Kiyonari and Brookes to be in with a shot of the title. Going into the final round, both riders were handily placed to kick for home but any hopes Brookes had of being the first Australian since Troy Bayliss in 1999 to win in BSB were thwarted by Kiyo's last round hat trick as he added to his 2006 and 2007 crowns.

Josh Brookes		**Ryuichi Kiyonari**	
Number:	4	Number:	8
DOB:	28 April, 1983	DOB:	23 September, 1982
Lives:	Sydney, Australia	Lives:	Saitama, Japan
Races:	43	Races:	122
Wins:	5	Wins:	41
2009 Position:	4th British Superbike Championship	2009 Position:	11th World Superbike Championship

Relentless
Suzuki by TAS

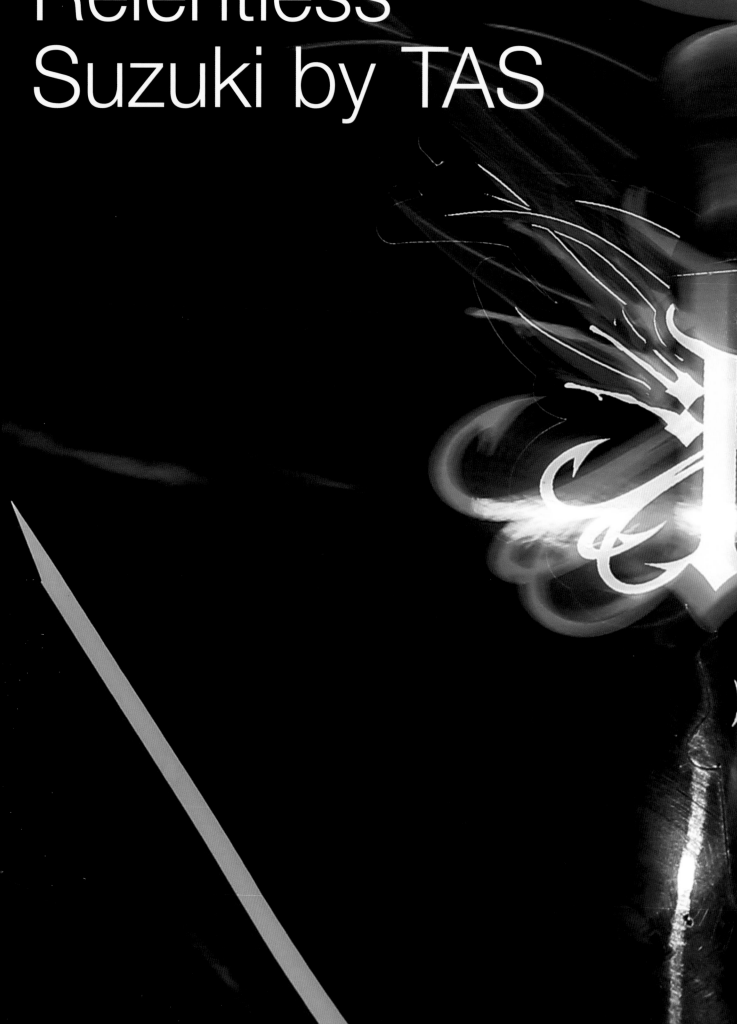

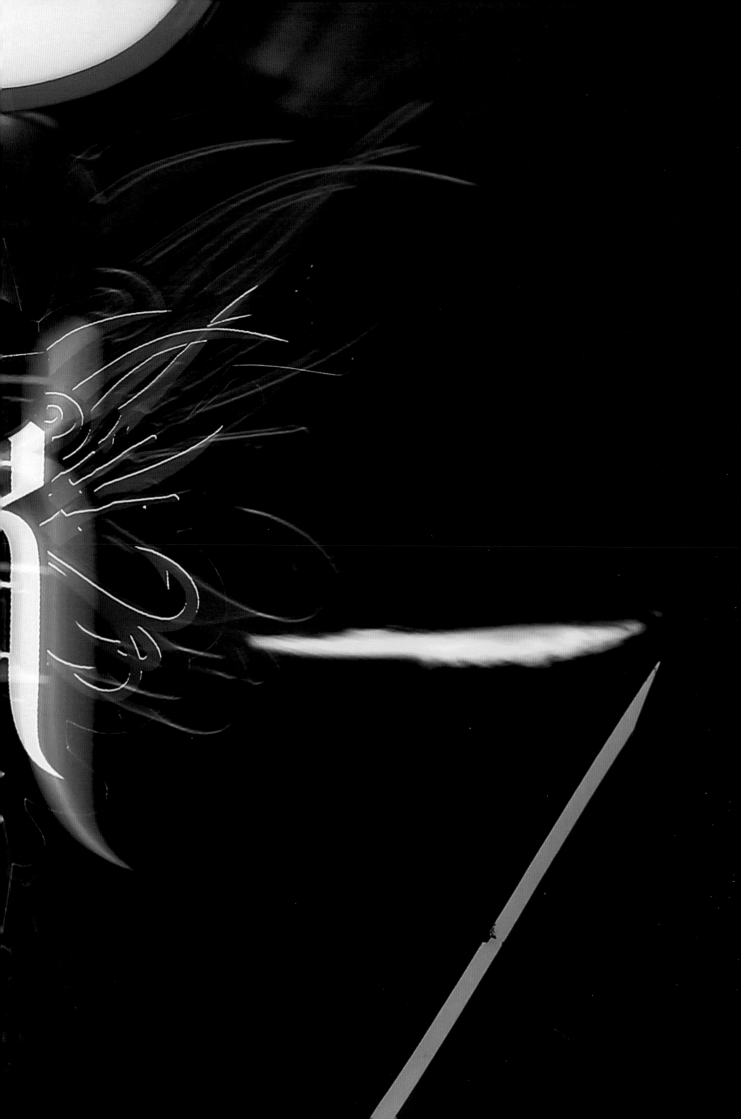

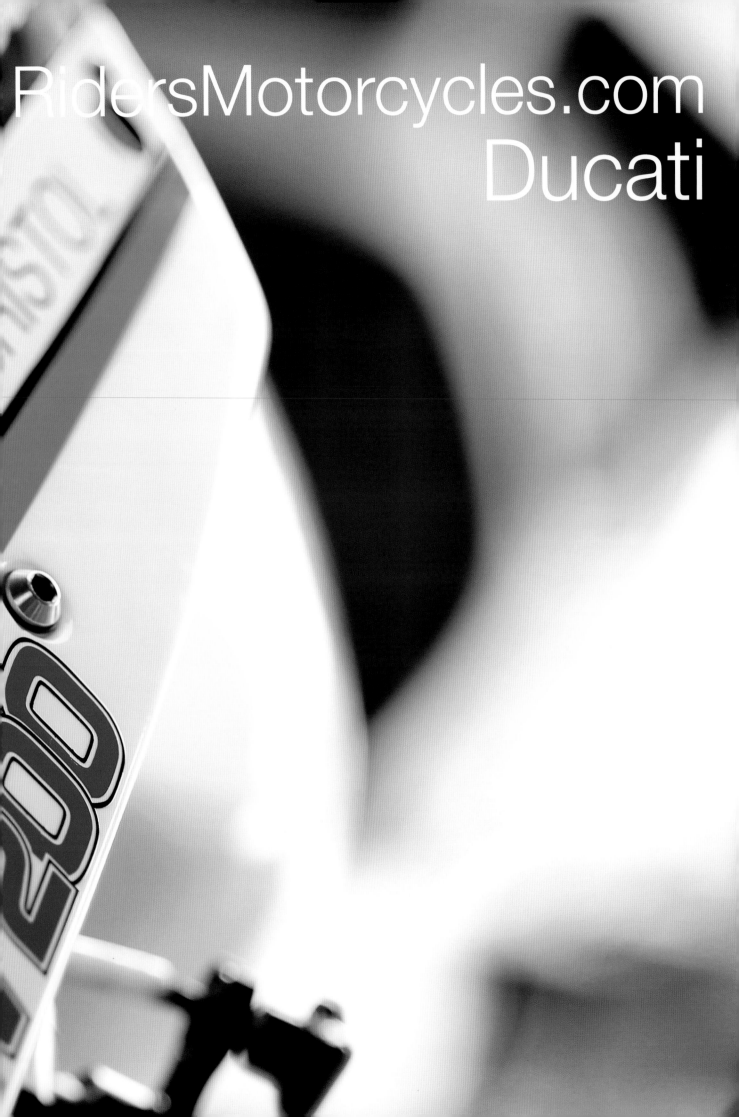

RidersMotorcycles.com Ducati

Machinery: Ducati 1098R
Owner: Phil Jessopp
Located: Bridgwater, Somerset
Pedigree: British Superbike & NW200 Race Winners

It seemed as though there may be a fairytale ending this season when the grand old master Michael Rutter hustled his Ducati into the Title Fight in a bid to land his first ever British Championship crown.

With rekindled spirit, the Rutter and Ducati combination ended up being a revelation this season and despite crashes at both Croft and Silverstone, he still had an outside chance going into Oulton but machine gremlins struck and his hopes were dashed. Team-mate Jessopp, injured at Mallory, made his comeback at Oulton from a badly broken leg but irrespective of how it all ended up, they won many fans this season who admired their efforts.

Michael Rutter

Number:	6
DOB:	18 April, 1972
Lives:	Bridgwater, Somerset
Races:	347
Wins:	27
2009 Position:	16th British Superbike Championship

Martin Jessopp

Number:	40
DOB:	04 November, 1985
Lives:	Yeovil, Somerset
Races:	55
Wins:	0
2009 Position:	3rd British Superbike Cup

MSS Colchester Kawasaki

Motorpoint Yamaha

Machinery: Yamaha YZF-R1
Principal: Rob McElnea
Located: Scunthorpe, North Lincolnshire
Pedigree: British Superbike Champions 1996, 1997 & 1998

A mixed season by anyone's standards which saw no less than five different riders involved aboard last year's all-conquering Yamaha R1 for Rob McElnea's longstanding BSB team.

With winter signing Neil Hodgson being forced to retire after a first round crash, in came Ian Lowry for a couple of rounds. He was replaced by ex World Supersport Champion Andrew Pitt who was subsequently sidelined after a nasty crash mid-season. Thereafter, in came French sensation Loris Baz to race alongside talented British youngster Dan Linfoot and between them, they finished the season very strongly.

Dan Linfoot		Loris Baz	
Number:	99	Number:	65
DOB:	08 July, 1988	DOB:	01 February, 1993
Lives:	Knaresborough, North Yorkshire	Lives:	Sallanches, France
Races:	31	Races:	7
Wins:	0	Wins:	0
2009 Position:	7th British Supersport Championship	2009 Position:	8th Superstock 1000
	36th British Superbike Championship		FIM Cup

Other riders: Neil Hodgson, Ian Lowry, Andrew Pitt

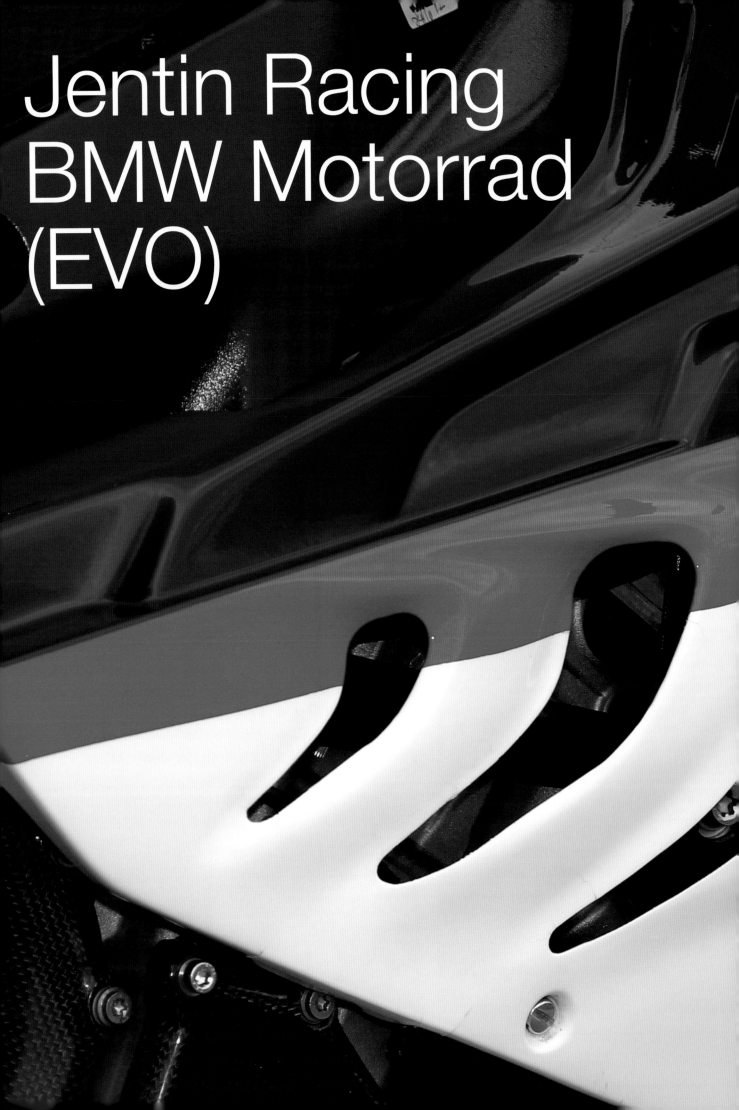

Jentin Racing
BMW Motorrad
(EVO)

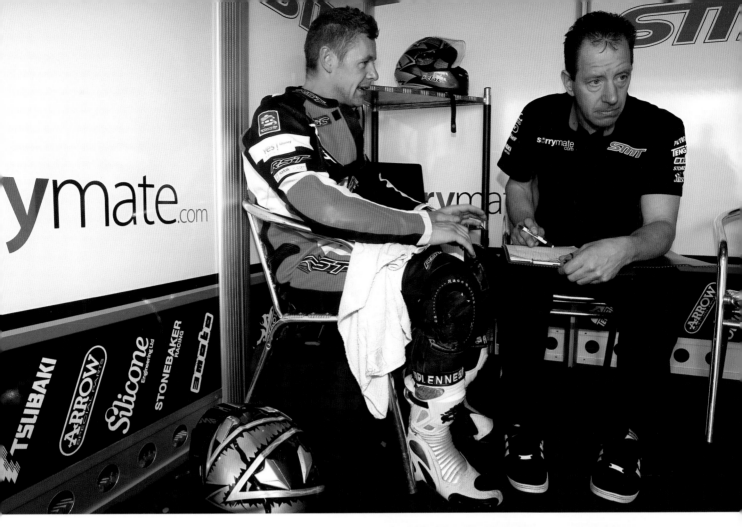

Ultimate Racing

Machinery: Yamaha YZF-R1
Owners: Ian Drake, David & Peter Hickman
Located: Alford, Lincolnshire
Pedigree: British Superbike Cup Runners-up 2009

Another family affair running on a tight budget which belied the efforts and results gained on track and testament to their prowess that Peter Hickman finished the season inside the top 20.

Despite his junior years, Hickman has plenty of Superbike experience and has weighed in with some great end of season performances in both qualifying and races to mix it up at the cutting edge. He is now well placed going into next season with the experiences gained during this one.

Peter Hickman

Number:	60
DOB:	8 April, 1987
Lives:	Alford, Lincolnshire
Races:	94
Wins:	0
2009 Position:	2nd in British Superbike Cup
	22nd British Superbike Championship

Doodson Motorsport Honda

Machinery: Honda CBR1000RR Fireblade
Owner: Tom Tunstall
Located: Denby Dale, West Yorkshire
Pedigree: British Superbike Cup Podium Finishers

One of the friendliest teams in the paddock and a true privateer entry in as much as friends and family are involved in the whole effort, but very much professional when it comes to presentation and results.

With world championship experience, the affable Tom Tunstall scored points in the last nine rounds, including a season's best points haul in the Oulton Park finale to hoist himself up the order and in doing so, rewarded his hardworking team and loyal sponsors.

Tom Tunstall

Number:	21
DOB:	21 June, 1978
Lives:	Huddersfield, West Yorkshire
Races:	99
Wins:	0
2009 Position:	4th British Superbike Cup
	30th British Superbike Championship

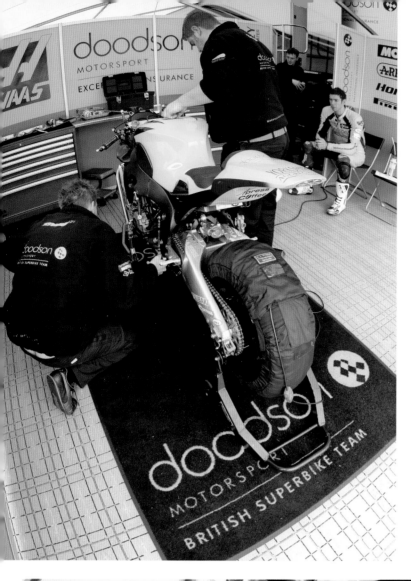

Redline KTM (EVO)

Machinery: KTM RC8R
Principal: Tim Walker
Located: Loughborough, Leicestershire
Pedigree: Debut Season in BSB

New into the BSB series this year, Redline Motorcycles continued to support their local rider James Edmeades but it was a far from smooth ride all round. The booming V-twin may have had a distinctive sound but Edmeades struggled to tame the Austrian beast and had more than his fair share of injuries which saw him miss a number of rounds.

However, towards the end of the season, his results did improve, including a fine fifth place in the EVO class at Silverstone, to end up 13th in the rankings.

James Edmeades

Number:	18
DOB:	01 September, 1983
Lives:	Loughborough, Leics
Races:	14
Wins:	0
2009 Position:	5th KTM RC8 Super Cup

Other riders:
David Wood, Alex Lowes

MSVR behind the scenes

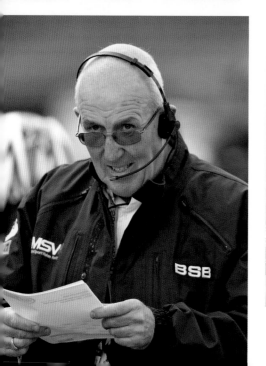

Tommy Hill - Worx Crescent Suzuki

Bruce Anstey - Relentless by TAS Suzuki

EVERYDAY IS A RACE DAY.

DIABLO ROSSO™ Corsa. Every bend is pure excitement. Stable in braking, precise in line, fast on exit and the throttle beckons to be opened again. A riding experience Pirelli brings to the road directly from the Superbike World Championship. From the

DIABLO
ROSSO CORSA

pirelli.com

Ryuichi Kiyonari - HM Plant Honda

Josh Brookes - HM Plant Honda

Troy Bayliss
III time World Superbike Champion

rear tyre's three zone differentiated compound and EPT technology that optimizes the contact patch, exceptional performance is guaranteed both on the road and on the track. Diablo Rosso Corsa: every day is a race day.

POWER IS NOTHING WITHOUT CONTROL

Circuit Maps

2010 British Superbike Series

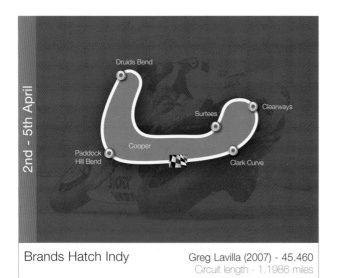

2nd - 5th April

Brands Hatch Indy
Greg Lavilla (2007) - 45.460
Circuit length - 1.1986 miles

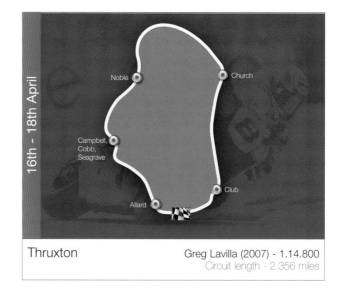

16th - 18th April

Thruxton
Greg Lavilla (2007) - 1.14.800
Circuit length - 2.356 miles

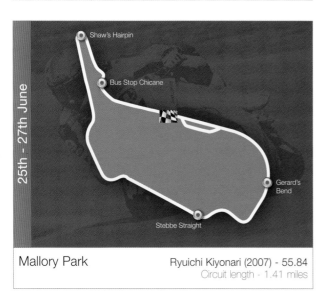

25th - 27th June

Mallory Park
Ryuichi Kiyonari (2007) - 55.84
Circuit length - 1.41 miles

2nd - 4th July

Knockhill
Shane Byrne (2006) - 47.474
Circuit length - 1.2713 miles

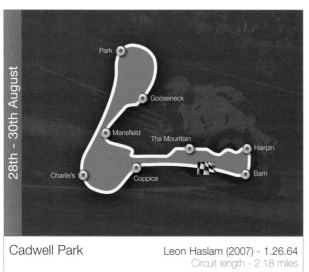

28th - 30th August

Cadwell Park
Leon Haslam (2007) - 1.26.64
Circuit length - 2.18 miles

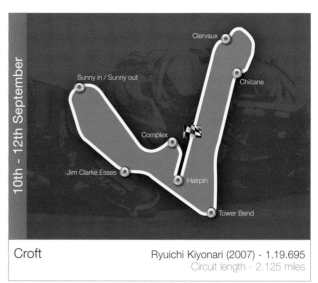

10th - 12th September

Croft
Ryuichi Kiyonari (2007) - 1.19.695
Circuit length - 2.125 miles

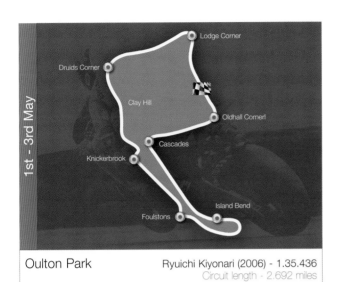

Lodge Corner
Druids Corner
Clay Hill
Oldhall Cornerl
Cascades
Knickerbrook
Island Bend
Foulstons

Oulton Park   Ryuichi Kiyonari (2006) - 1.35.436
                     Circuit length - 2.692 miles

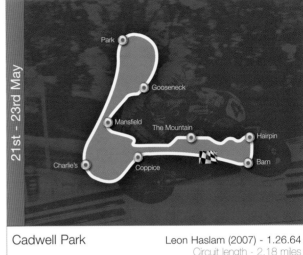

Park
Gooseneck
Mansfield
The Mountain
Hairpin
Charlie's
Coppice
Barn

Cadwell Park   Leon Haslam (2007) - 1.26.64
                     Circuit length - 2.18 miles

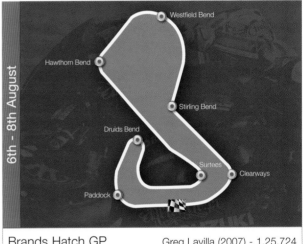

The Esses
Sear Corner
Senna Straight
Coram Curve
Riches Corner
Russell Bend

Snetterton   Ryuichi Kiyonari (2007) - 1.04.688
                     Circuit length - 1.952 miles

Westfield Bend
Hawthorn Bend
Stirling Bend
Druids Bend
Surtees
Clearways
Paddock

Brands Hatch GP   Greg Lavilla (2007) - 1.25.724
                     Circuit length - 2.3009 miles

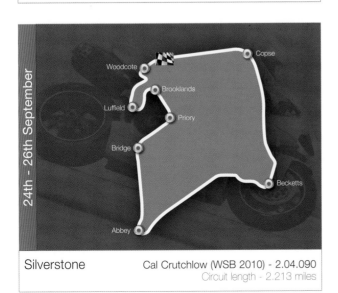

Copse
Woodcote
Brooklands
Luffield
Priory
Bridge
Becketts
Abbey

Silverstone   Cal Crutchlow (WSB 2010) - 2.04.090
                     Circuit length - 2.213 miles

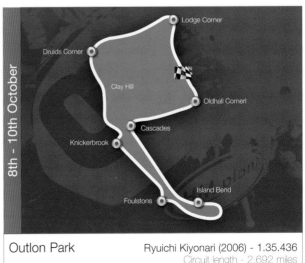

Lodge Corner
Druids Corner
Clay Hill
Oldhall Cornerl
Cascades
Knickerbrook
Island Bend
Foulstons

Outlon Park   Ryuichi Kiyonari (2006) - 1.35.436
                     Circuit length - 2.692 miles

ROUND
01
Brands Hatch Indy
2nd - 5th April

Thruxton
16th - 18th April

MAIDEN VICTORY JOY FOR BROOKES...

The victories were shared by series leader Tommy Hill along with Josh Brookes, who shook off his 'bad-boy' image of the previous year with a strong and stylish ride to enjoy the BSB winner's champagne for the first time. But all of that was overshadowed by a serious injury sustained by James Ellison during the previous day's practice.

The Swan Honda rider had been running at lap record pace during Friday's free practice and was maintaining that speed into the Saturday morning's third and final session when he highsided through the long, sweeping Goodwood right-hander. Ellison sustained a broken right femur before undergoing surgery later in the day to pin the bone.

It was his team-mate Stuart Easton who made the early running in the opening race before being overhauled by Worx Suzuki's Yukio Kagayama but soon Brookes was ahead on his HM Plant Honda with Hill on the other Worx Suzuki chasing him down. Going into the Club chicane on the penultimate lap, Hill timed his move to perfection to grab the lead and take the race.

Brookes held off Kagayama in a final slipstreaming battle to take second while Easton was fourth ahead of the RidersMotorcycles.com Ducati duo of Michael Rutter and the quickly developing Martin Jessopp. Jessopp's somewhat surprising pace was rewarded with pole start for the second race, though he was quickly outgunned by the rampant Brookes.

The Australian forged clear from the start with Hill never far behind and trying everything he knew to find a way through in a race long duel which narrowly ended in favour of Brookes. It was not only Brookes' first in the series, but the first for his team in two years and the first by an Aussie in the series since Troy Bayliss won at Cadwell Park in 1999.

"I always knew that I was capable of doing this and now I have a trophy to prove it," enthused Brookes, adding "It feels pretty good; I've waited a long time for this moment." The consolation for Hill was that he increased his lead in the standings. Easton took third ahead of Ryuichi Kiyonari, Jessopp and Michael Laverty.

David Anthony, riding for MIST Suzuki, took the victories in the BSB-EVO class, with Steve Brogan, the opening round double winner, having to race in the main championship while technical issues to his BMW were resolved in line with series regulations.

BSB Championship Positions

1	HILL	90
2	BROOKES	56
3	EASTON	50
4	ELLISON	41
5	SEELEY	40
6	KIYONARI	40

BSB-EVO Championship Positions

1	ANTHONY	74
2	KENNAUGH	56
3	BURNS	53
4	BROGAN	50
5	D JOHNSON	50
6	G JOHNSON	40

The Power of ®WORX
with Lithium Technology

LITHIUM POWER

POWERSHARE ™
The power to share

LITHIUM POWER 18V

For the full range of Worx products please go to:

worxtools.com

Official title sponsor
of the British Superbike Team

WORX SUZUKI
you've got the power

ROUND

03
Oulton Park

1st - 3rd May

Above: Chris Walker rode the MSS Colchester Kawasaki, deputising for the injured Si Andrews

Top right: Michael Laverty in the classic shot at Lodge

Far right: And they're off!! The riders leave the line

Right: Aboard the Buildbase Kawasaki, John Laverty leads brother Michael, Alastair Seeley and Josh Brookes

ROUND
04
Cadwell Park
21st - 23rd May

Above: Alastair Seeley heads the pack into the bottom of the mountain

Left: Tommy Hill takes the fast, un-spectacular route over the mountain

Right: It was Ian Lowry's turn to step onto Rob Mac's Motorpoint Yamaha

Left: Michael Laverty takes the spectacular route over the mountain

Right: Swan Honda's Stuart Easton had a tough time at Cadwell while (**below**) Josh Brookes had a much better time taking the race two win at HM Plant Honda's local circuit

Above: Michael Laverty on his way to two more solid podium results

Left: Yukio Kagayama holds a tight line, but crashed out of race one and ruled himself out of race two

Sequence: Yukio Kagayama crashes out in spectacular style

Below: Easton had a mixed bag of results while Ellison was still recovering from the broken femur sustained at Thruxton in round two

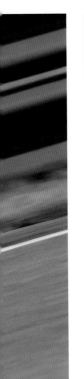 

Mallory Park
25th - 27th June

KIYONARI AT THE DOUBLE FROM BROOKES ...

A s World Cup fans watched the nauseous encounter between England and Germany on the big screens, Ryuichi Kiyonari was in scintillating form as he completed his first double of the campaign, in each race running clear of his HM Plant Honda team-mate Josh Brookes who shrugged aside the controversial incident of his previous visit to the Leicestershire circuit to turn on the style.

Kiyonari, who has something of a love-hate relationship with the circuit, knew that this time around everything was going his way as he took his second pole of the campaign by bettering his own lap record ahead of an opening race which was red flagged after four laps because of a heavy crash involving Martin Jessopp, who sustained a broken leg, and Dan Linfoot.

Michael Laverty set the pace on the restart but a third of the way into the race, the Relentless Suzuki rider was overhauled by Brookes, but the Australian led for only a handful of laps before Kiyonari was out front, taking the victory by a little under two seconds. Brookes took some consolation for being second best as he clawed points back on Tommy Hill whose Worx Suzuki had been sidelined by clutch problems.

James Ellison, making his comeback from injury, ran bravely in 13th position, and next time out he went one better, reflecting: "I did the best I could possibly do and scored points. I was feeling physically tired towards the end of the races which is something that I am not used to so that is frustrating for me."

At least he finished both encounters. His Swan Honda team-mate Stuart Easton, fifth in the opener, clipped a kerb at the Bus Stop and tumbled, as Kiyonari, second on the opening lap to the local favourite Chris Walker riding a privately entered Suzuki, asserted himself to be leading next time around with Brookes soon running second having accounted for both Michael Laverty and Michael Rutter. Walker, having his best day at the races for some time, took fifth place ahead of Buildbase Kawasaki's John Laverty.

Hill was again struggling, running back in eighth place, and seeing his lead in the title stakes eroded by Brookes but in contrast, in the BSB-EVO class, Hudson Kennaugh, with a second and first, was increasing his advantage over Steve Brogan who having won the first race, fell in a tangle at the chicane next time out.

BSB Championship Positions

#	Rider	Points
1	HILL	154
2	BROOKES	150
3	M LAVERTY	133
4	KIYONARI	128
5	RUTTER	114
6	J LAVERTY	98

BSB-EVO Championship Positions

#	Rider	Points
1	KENNAUGH	187
2	BROGAN	161
3	D JOHNSON	112
4	PEKKANEN	106
5	ANTHONY	103
6	ZANOTTI	96

All torque and looking for action?

You've seen it for the first time on British circuits in 2010, now you can be part of the action in the 2011 Harley-Davidson® XR1200® Trophy.

- Nine races at seven British Superbike rounds
- Harley-Davidson XR1200® – developed by Harris Performance
- Partnership with Dunlop Tyres

- Live TV and recorded highlights coverage
- An affordable way to rub shoulders with the BSB teams in the pit

For further information about the series, sponsorship enquiries or to register your interest, please contact the Harley-Davidson XR1200® Trophy team on
xr1200trophy@rbpinternational.com
www.harley-davidson.co.uk/xr1200trophy

Make every day count

©H-D 2010. Harley, Harley-Davidson and the Bar and Shield logo are among the trademarks of H-D Michigan, LLC.

ROUND
06
Knockhill
2nd - 4th July

Right: The sign says it all as torrential rain disrupted Scotland's only BSB round

Below: Interesting lines through Duffus Dip on lap one of the race one restart

Far right: Tommy Hill powers his Worx Suzuki over the crest at the start/finish

Left: Michael Rutter takes in the joy of his first race win on the RidersMotorcycles.com Ducati

Above: Josh Brookes joins in the Scottish spirit then takes things somewhat more seriously as he leads the pack through turn one (right)

Sequence: Carnage as a number of riders succumb to the slippery conditions leading to the stoppage of race two, and the eventual cancellation of BSB events for the rest of the day.

Far right: Tommy Hill on the limit

Knockhill
2nd - 4th July

RAIN MASTER RUTTER TRIUMPHS BUT WEATHER WINS THE DAY ...

Michael Rutter took the victory in the opening race that was completed at the third attempt on a weather-ravaged Scottish Sunday afternoon which eventually thwarted the determined efforts of everyone involved to complete the meeting as torrential rain and gusting winds made any further racing impossible.

Practice and qualifying at the Fife circuit had been run in perfect conditions with Josh Brookes powering to his first pole start of the campaign for HM Plant Honda but race day dawned with pouring rain and in a 20-minute wet session it was James Ellison, three months on from breaking his femur, who ran his Swan Honda fastest.

Brookes took the early lead as racing began, hotly pursued by Rutter aboard the RidersMotorcycles.com Ducati with Ellison running third but they had barely completed the first of the scheduled 30 laps before a heavy downpour made conditions unsafe and the red flags were out.

Up against time after the lengthy delay, the race restarted but to be decided over 20 laps, yet on the third lap, Dan Linfoot lost control of his Motorpoint Yamaha with the bike careering on downhill and collecting the luckless Chris Walker, bringing out the red flags again, both to deal with the incident and to clean the mud off the circuit.

And so it was third time lucky. Brookes made the early running from Rutter, Kiyonari and Ellison. But Kiyo was hungry for better, attacking Rutter to go second on the fifth lap and next time around he was leading from his team-mate Brookes. Rutter was having none of it and upped his game, taking Brookes to go second at two-thirds distance and then got the better of Kiyonari to take his first victory in two years by half a second.

Brookes finished third and moved into the lead in the title stakes as Tommy Hill ran eighth on his Worx Suzuki and his hopes of reversing that in the second race ended as the red flags came out again with six riders going down on the first corner of the first lap as more heavy rain fell bringing the abandonment of the meeting.

Gary Johnson, riding the AIM Suzuki, took his first victory in the BSB-EVO class, ahead of Two Brothers Kawasaki rider David Johnson as Hudson Kennaugh took fifth in class, two places up on Steve Brogan.

BSB Championship Positions		BSB-EVO Championship Positions	
1 BROOKES	166	1 KENNAUGH	198
2 HILL	162	2 BROGAN	170
3 KIYONARI	148	3 D JOHNSON	132
4 M LAVERTY	146	4 PEKKANEN	116
5 RUTTER	139	5 G JOHNSON	116
6 J LAVERTY	108	6 ZANOTTI	109

BMW Motorrad

S 1000 RR

BMW

The Ultimate
Riding Machine

TROPHIES?
WE'RE SEEING DOUBLE.

Jon Kirkham, Steve Brogan and the BMW S 1000 RR. This season, they were an
explosive combination. We'd like to thank the Samsung Mobile Racing and Jentin
Racing-BMW Motorrad teams and all their sponsors for a great year. With wins
in both the Metzeler National Superstock 1000 and Mirror.co.uk EVO Superbike
categories, we're pretty sure our first BSB Championships won't be our last.

To test ride the S 1000 RR, call 0800 777 155, visit bmw-motorrad.co.uk
or contact your nearest BMW Motorrad dealer.

S 1000 RR
UNSTOPPABLE SPORT

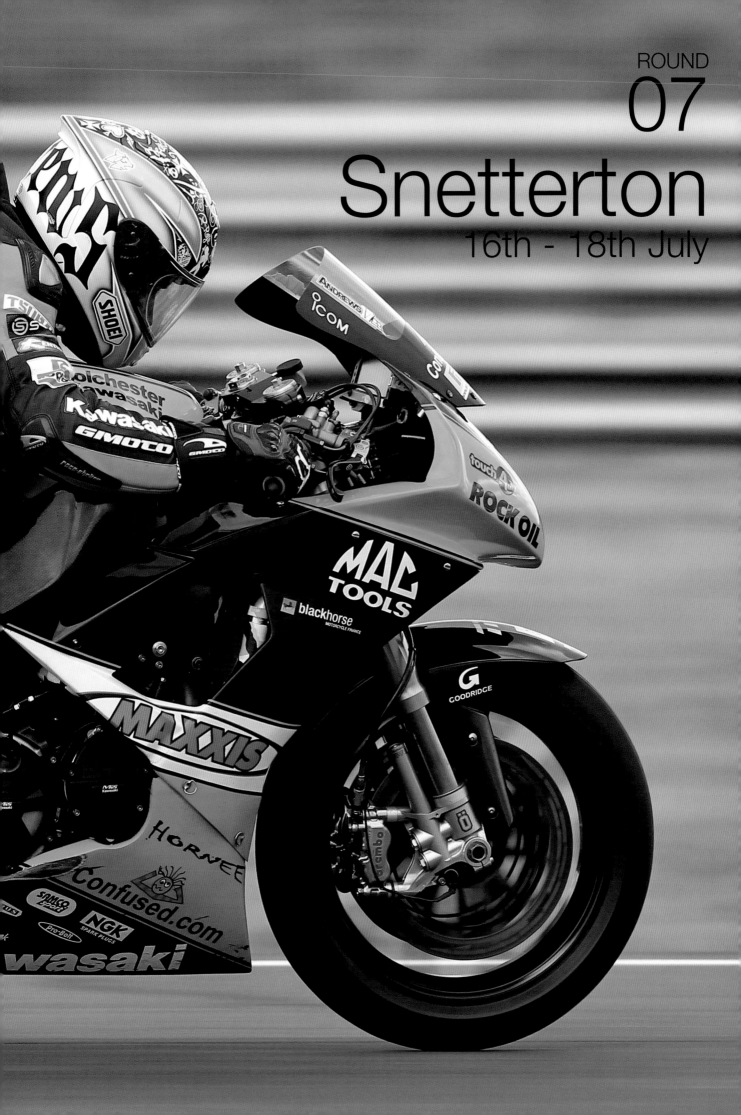

ROUND
07
Snetterton
16th - 18th July

Left: A cautious start for Kiyonari as Rutter gains the advantage off the line

Bottom left: Easton and Andrews do battle at close quarters

Above: John Laverty looking stylish through Russells – the only left handed corner on the circuit where riders are on the gas

Top left: Brookes sweeping through Richies

Far left: Chris Walker exits the shadows under the bridge

Left: Ellison gets on the gas

Left: Brookes celebrates his race one win

Above: Steve Plater was still recovering from the injuries sustained in a 100+mph accident at the NW200 and made an 'interesting' debut as a 'brolly dolly'

Top right: Tommy Hill leads Rutter, Seeley and Michael Laverty through Russells

Right: Everyone gets cleanly through Richies on lap one

HENDERSON

INSURANCE BROKERS

Leading independent regional broker with local representation ensuring the highest level of client service

Bespoke solutions for all commercial insurance requirements

Henderson Insurance Brokers Limited has grown to 11 nationwide offices in its 24-year history

More than 300 staff work for the company to provide advice in a clear and precise way

Henderson provide a wide range of specialist divisions that cover every type of business:

Retail • Construction • Haulage • Professional Indemnity • Healthcare • Corporate • Surety Services • Risk Management • Manufacturing • UK Credit

Henderson Insurance Brokers Limited
Trueman House, Capitol Park, Leeds, LS27 0TS
Tel: 0113 393 6300 • Fax: 0113 393 6376

www.hibl.co.uk

Authorised and Regulated by the Financial Services Authority

ROUND
10
Croft
10th - 12th September

Top left: HM Plant Honda's Josh Brookes heads through the trees into the Jim Clarke Esses

Bottom left: Michael Laverty leads the pack into turn one on his way to a race two victory

Above: Swan Honda team mates, Ellison and Easton battle at close quarters into the hairpin

Left: Tommy Hill chases Michael Laverty. The first two podium places in both races were shared out between them

Bottom left: Kiyonari had a poor day by his standards with an eleventh place in race one and a fourth in race two

Left: Rutter had an even worse day with 23rd in race one but a stronger outing in race two

Below: Seeley tangled with Gary Mason at the hairpin and ended up in the gravel

Above: Motorpoint Yamaha's Dan Linfoot had a respectable day with a fifth place in race one

Left: Rutter tipped off in race one, remounting to finish in 23rd place

Right: Kiyonari turns on the style in race two

Croft
10th - 12th September

FIRST BLOOD TO HILL AND LAVERTY IN TITLE FIGHT …

Tommy Hill and Michael Laverty fully justified their Title Fighters status in two hard fought races as they each took a win and a second place amid some superb front-running while their rivals struggled to find their form in these opening two races of the final seven-race Showdown for the crown.

Hill put his Worx Suzuki onto pole for the fifth time but that counted for little as he was outgunned at the start by the determined Laverty and after an early intervention by the safety car as David Johnson's spectacular highside was dealt with, Hill found the extra pace to take the lead on the fifth lap.

"I had to work hard to keep Michael behind me," explained Hill, adding: "I was panicking a bit over the last few laps but I had the lead and just had to keep it consistent because I knew that Michael would be there. I was protecting my lines and just tried to keep my cool but I did what I needed to do and this win was just what we needed."

Laverty crossed the line just 0.155 seconds down on Hill but of the other Title Fighters, Josh Brookes struggled with handling issues and could only manage sixth and his HM Plant Honda team-mate Ryuichi Kiyonari overcame a poor qualifying position to finish 11th. Alastair Seeley and Michael Rutter both tumbled out such was the drama.

Once again, Laverty was quickly away at the start of the second race and although Hill reeled him in and overtook him, this time the Relentless Suzuki rider bit back to take his second victory of the campaign.

"I was not going to give up and put in two hard laps to get him back," explained Laverty, adding: "I was prepared to fight back and that brought me the win." Hill ran 0.202 seconds down on him as Kiyonari came through to finish fourth ahead of Rutter while Alastair Seeley struggled back in 15th place.

Of the rest, Stuart Easton had the best results netting a brace of third places for Swan Honda at their local track while Simon Andrews, fourth in the opener on the MSS Colchester Kawasaki, enjoyed his best BSB result as did Dan Linfoot who ran strongly on his Motorpoint Yamaha to cross the line just adrift of him.

In the BSB-EVO class, the engine issues around the Splitlath Aprilias had been resolved with Hudson Kennaugh taking a winning double while Steve Brogan maintained his points lead with second and third placings on the Jentin BMW despite injury.

BSB Championship Positions

1	HILL	570
2	M LAVERTY	554
3	KIYONARI	543
4	BROOKES	542
5	RUTTER	521
6	SEELEY	506

BSB-EVO Championship Positions

1	BROGAN	356
2	KENNAUGH	322
3	G JOHNSON	278
4	ZANOTTI	237
5	PEKKANEN	234
6	D JOHNSON	200

Riders

www.ridersmotorcycles.com

Three destinations, one passion...

...and we've been fulfilling that same red blooded, two wheeled passion
to our fellow Ducatisti, riders and racers throughout the UK since 1976.
Our experience in everything Ducati is second to none, from fitting
new brake pads on a Monster to preparing our own BSB race team
bikes. Riders, discover why experience really counts.

BRIDGWATER   tel: **01278 457 652**
BRISTOL   tel: **0117 958 8777**
CARDIFF   tel: **02920 780070**
enquiries@ridersmotorcycles.com

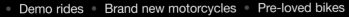

• Demo rides • Brand new motorcycles • Pre-loved bikes
• Full servicing facilities • Factory trained technicians • Race preparation & set-up
• Casual clothing & riding apparel • Official Ducati Performance Parts and Accessories

ROUND

11 Silverstone

24th - 26th September

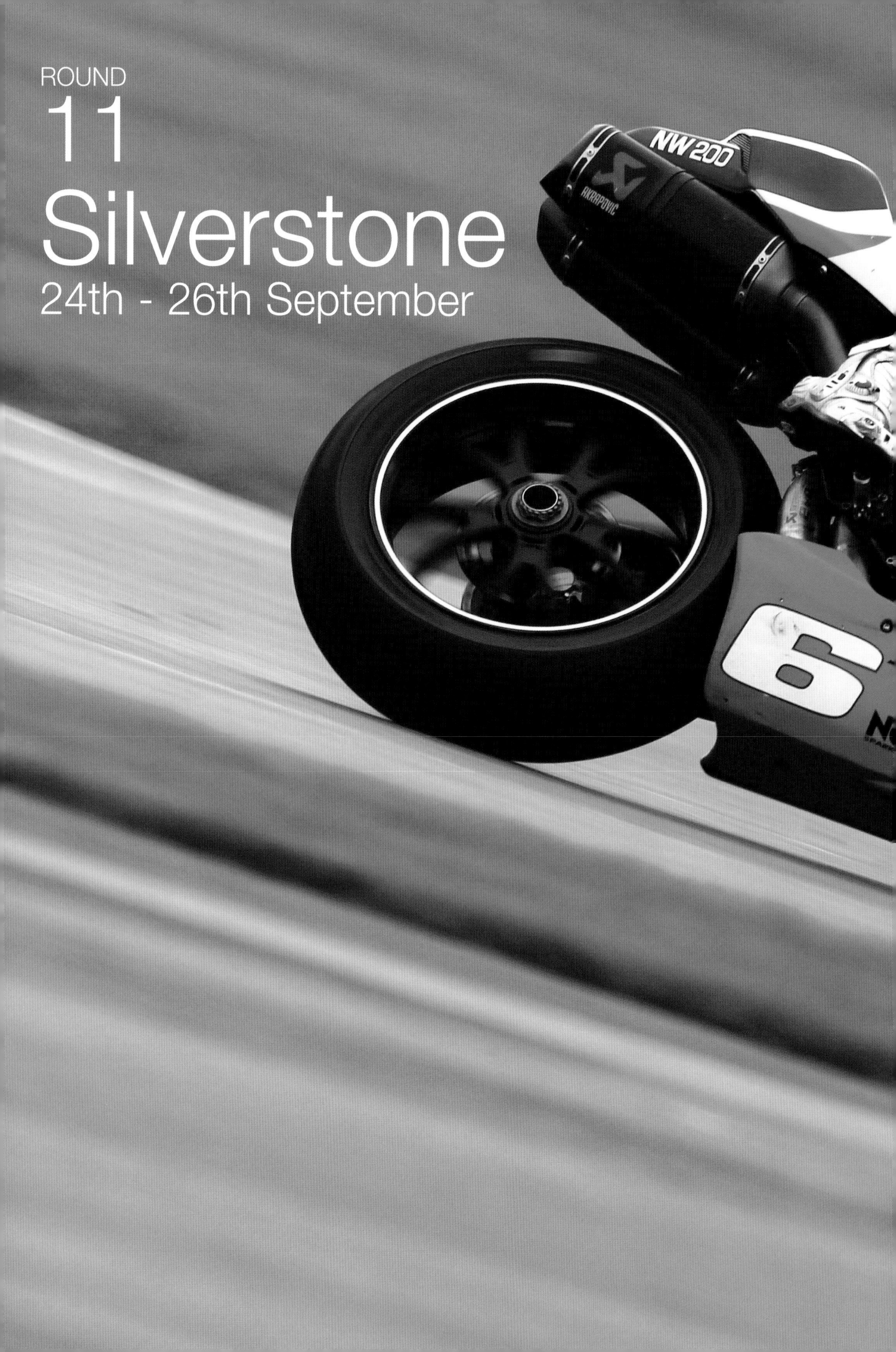

Mirror.co.uk BSB-EVO

BROGAN GIVES BMW INAUGURAL EVO GLORY ...

The inaugural Mirror.co.uk British Superbike Evo Championship saw a titanic battle between Steve Brogan on the Jentin Racing BMW and Hudson Kennaugh, who started the year on the MAR Racing Kawasaki before switching mid-season to the Splitlath Aprilia. Both had to overcome technical problems, controversy and protest but the title went right down to the very last race with Brogan coming out on top by just 3 points.

Brogan's season started well with a double victory at the opening round but a technical issue with the BMW made him ineligible for points at Thruxton and he immediately lost 50 points to his rivals. However, with more wins than anyone else (12), he was able to make up the ground and edge clear although disappointing results at Brands Hatch and Silverstone meant that Kennaugh came into the final round only eight points adrift.

The South African's year was also somewhat turbulent when he surprisingly left the MAR Racing team in June to join the Splitlath squad. The Aprilia was still very much unproven and Kennaugh's title aspirations were dealt a huge blow when he had to withdraw from the Cadwell Park round after an administrative error led to a part on the Italian machine being declared illegal.

That handed the initiative to former National Superstock Champion Brogan and with a 48-point lead, the title was seemingly his. However, a determined Kennaugh won 4 of the last 8 races, finishing on the podium in the others, to set up a last race showdown. The ever-smiling Brogan needed to finish in second place in the final race to take the crown though and he duly achieved this to take his second major title in three years – though not before surviving a last minute protest from the Splitlath team!

Leading road racer Gary Johnson (AIM Suzuki) just failed to catch the leading duo and had it not been for a slightly sluggish start to the season, the Lincolnshire rider could well have made it a three-way dice for the Championship. However, four no-scores in the first eight races meant that the 30-year old was playing catch up for the rest of the season and although he ultimately ran out of races, he impressed greatly, particularly in the wet, with two wins and thirteen podiums more than proving his short circuit capabilities.

Behind the leading trio, Finnish rider Pauli Pekkanen completed his third different championship in successive years and, after competing in European Superstock and KTM Super Cup in 2008 and 2009 respectively, he made a successful switch to the Superbike class. The 27-year-old got quicker as the year progressed and a flurry of late season rostrums elevated him to fourth place overall.

Other race winners included early season pace setter David Anthony, the Australian only competing in the first few rounds for the MIST Suzuki team, and Chris Burns on the second Splitlath Aprilia while consistent performances by Aaron Zanotti and David Johnson saw them finish in fifth and sixth respectively in the final Championship table.

Championship Positions

1	Steve BROGAN	431
2	Hudson KENNAUGH	428
3	Gary JOHNSON	340
4	Pauli PEKKANEN	306
5	Aaron ZANOTTI	275
6	David JOHNSON	200

Metzeler National Superstock 600 Championship

IT'S A BEAUTIFUL DAY FOR JOSH …

The battle for the Metzeler National Superstock 600cc Championship was nothing short of superb and with fortunes fluctuating throughout the season, it all came down to a final round showdown between no less than four riders. The title changed hands on practically each and every one of the 12 laps at Oulton Park but eighth place was enough to see Josh Day seal the crown by just a single point with only seven points separating the top four riders in the final Championship table.

Day had led the Championship on the AIR Racing Yamaha since round four at Knockhill and with two more wins and podiums at the next four races he was able to open up a healthy 31-point lead. However, a run of relatively lowly finishes meant he failed to finish on the podium in the final six races but, with Danny Buchan only picking up fourth at the final round, the eighth place was enough to see him follow in the footsteps of some illustrious names who have emerged from a series that continues to provide excitement of the highest order.

Buchan, like Day, put together a run of five podiums in six races on his MSS Colchester Kawasaki, which included wins at Snetterton and Brands Hatch, but no-scores at Cadwell and Croft severely dented his challenge. With Day back down the field, second place at Oulton would have been enough for him to clinch the title but when he had an off-track excursion towards the end of the race, his hopes disappeared.

Buchan finished the season in third overall as fellow Kawasaki rider Luke Stapleford sneaked through into second, courtesy of winning that final round at Oulton. A steady start to the season meant that Stapleford didn't come into title contention until the last few rounds but two wins and a second in the final three races saw him come oh so close to catching Day and it was he who finished a point adrift with Buchan a further three points behind.

Irishman John Simpson also had a slim chance of taking the Championship at Oulton and although he took second, the disqualifications he'd suffered earlier in the season at Brands Hatch and Croft were ultimately what cost him dearly and he had to settle for fourth overall albeit only eight points behind Day!

Fifth placed Jimmy Hill and Nikki Coates were the only other riders to win races during the season whilst Adam Lyon, Connor Behan, Matt Bilton, Josh Wainwright, Johnny Blackshaw, Daniel Kinloch, Robbie Stewart, Freddie Russo and John Dean all got to stand on the podium at least once in what was another highly competitive season in the class that continues to breed the stars of tomorrow.

Championship Positions

1	Josh DAY (Yamaha)	155
2	Luke STAPLEFORD (Kawasaki)	154
3	Danny BUCHAN (Kawasaki)	151
4	John SIMPSON (Triumph)	147
5	Jimmy HILL (Triumph)	133
6	Adam Lyon (Yamaha)	86

SpeedyRetail.com British 125GP Championship

Incorporating the ACU Academy Cup

LODGE COMES OUT ON TOP...

Just as it had been in previous seasons, the SpeedyRetail.com 125GP Championship was again one of the closest, and coming in to the final round at Oulton Park, James Lodge, Deane Brown and Rob Guiver were all in with a chance of taking the number one plate. But, despite a terrible run of luck in the second half of the season, it was again Lodge who came out on top, the Yorkshire rider taking the title for the second successive year.

With three wins and a podium in the first five rounds, it looked as if Lodge was going to run away with it as his pace, particularly in qualifying, was leaving his rivals trailing in his wake, but he then suffered an horrendous run of form that saw him finish just two of the next six rounds. However, a vital second place at the penultimate round at Silverstone elevated him back to the top of the table and he was able to make it title number two with a calculated ride to fourth at Oulton.

Guiver, continuing with Steve Patrickson's SP125 team, took victories at Snetterton and Cadwell, which helped him overhaul Lodge but, crucially, he crashed out in the terrible conditions at Silverstone and he again had to settle for the bridesmaid position, just four points behind.

Scottish rider Brown was arguably the most consistent rider in the field, taking an impressive seven podiums and his debut win in the class, but DNFs at the first two rounds meant he was always playing catch up to his rivals and his charge ultimately came up short as he ended up equal on points with Guiver.

Taylor Mackenzie made further strides forward, taking three wins over the course of the year, and had it not been for crashes at Croft and Silverstone, he too could have been in with a chance of the title at the final round but he had to settle for fourth overall with John McPhee, race winner at Croft, one place further back after a strong run of form mid-season put him into contention also.

Fraser Rogers, Sam Hornsey, Edward Rendell, Andrew Reid and Philip Wakefield were just a number of other riders to impress at various stages of the season whilst Dakota Mamola, son of former GP legend Randy, was well to the fore in the selected rounds he contested, just missing out on the win at Snetterton.

Meanwhile, Brown had the consolation of winning the ACU Academy Cup, for riders aged between 13 and 16, from McPhee, Rogers, Lee Jackson, Hornsey and Reid.

Championship Positions			**Cup Positions**	
1	James LODGE (Honda)	149	1 Deane BROWN	173
2	Rob GUIVER (Honda)	145	2 John McPHEE	154.5
3	Deane BROWN (Honda)	145	3 Fraser ROGERS	145.5
4	Taylor MACKENZIE (Honda)	131	4 Lee JACKSON	121.5
5	John McPHEE (Honda)	100.5	5 Sam HORNSEY	117.5
6	Fraser ROGERS (Honda)	84	6 Andrew REID	114

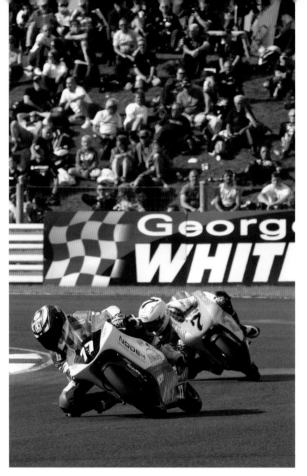

Henderson Harley-Davidson
XR1200 Trophy

MCWILLIAMS BACK TO HIS BEST ...

The Henderson Harley-Davidson XR1200 Trophy replaced the KTM RC8 Super Cup in 2010 as the premier one-make series to be held alongside the main British championship classes and it followed a similar pattern, a combination of seasoned veterans, young chargers and guest riders keeping the crowds entertained at each round.

The championship was supported by the manufacturer's dealer network in a seven-race series, which was held at four events, and it was former GP winner Jeremy McWilliams that came out on top, the 46-year-old Ulsterman winning no less than five of the seven races. Second in the other two, McWilliams was the class act of the field and took the title by a commanding 44 points.

It was another experienced campaigner that pushed McWilliams the hardest, Wigan's Mike Edwards more often than not finishing right on the tail of his rival. The multiple British champion took a solitary win at the final round at Cadwell and took five more podiums but a DNF in the penultimate race was enough to hand McWilliams the crown.

Double Scottish Superstock 1000cc champion Torquil Paterson was comfortably the best of the rest as he took three podiums and finished in the top five in every race and he was never too far behind the leading group. Leading Classic exponent Lea Gourlay was the only other race winner, taking a victory at Mallory Park, but his season ended with a serious practice crash at the Ulster GP and that allowed the consistent Darren James to finish in fourth overall just ahead of Ed Smith.

British Supersport Championship refugee James Webb took over from Sean Emmett, who retired after the first round, and he ended the year with two third place finishes to his name and sixth in the championship with the top ten being completed by Dijon Compton, Rhys 'Banzai' Boyd, Gary Byrne and Alex Gault.

Meanwhile, fans' favourite Guy Martin, American ace Roland Sands and British Superstock regular Matt Layt were just some of the other riders to have selected outings on the American machines.

Championship Positions

1	Jeremy McWILLIAMS	165
2	Mike EDWARDS	121
3	Torquil PATERSON	100
4	Darren JAMES	61
5	Ed SMITH	60
6	James WEBB	58